W9-CAA-349

YOUR SECOND CHILDHOOD

YOUR SECOND CHILDHOOD

verses by

LEONARD FEENEY

pictures by

Michael Cunningham

THE BRUCE PUBLISHING COMPANY
MILWAUKEE

Printed in the United States of
America

This book is produced in complete accord with the Government rules & regulations for the conservation of paper and other essential materials.

CONTENTS

EXHIBIT NUMBER ONE

Michael and I begin our book
By giving you a lyrical and pictorial look
At a little old lady with large eyes,
Whose purpose it is to illustrate surprise:
Whose eyes were intended to let others see
Just what complete astonishment can be.

At three score and seven she spends her
spinsterhood
By sometimes being appreciated, sometimes
misunderstood,
Because it is noticed that she never SEES
a thing merely,
But must STARE at it questioningly
and queerly,
With eyelids wide apart, and pupils dilated,
With arms extended, and breath abated,
As though it had that instant been created;

As though it were impossible to be sure
a cat's a cat,
a sofa furniture;

That any clock could tinkle half past seven;
That flowers could be in gardens,
stars in Heaven,

And, of course, that any visitor could
come to pay a call:
In fact that there could ever be anything
at all.

MR. PUSBY

Mr. Pusby likes to wear
Overalls
Everywhere
In the living room,
and halls,
And on the stair;

Going in and out of doors,
Not merely when he's doing chores
Which require
Overalls, but when he's doing
anything:

Listening to a lady sing,

Or merely sitting by the fire.

The doctors have examined him to see

Just what his malady can be,
And found that Mr. Pusby has what
Science calls
A strong desire to keep on wearing
overalls.

THE OLD SMOKER

Old Mr. McNally
Sits on a doorstep in Grogan's Alley,
Day after day
With a pipe in his hand;
And the reason he sits there specifi-cally
Is hard to say,
And harder to understand.
He doesn't indulge in conversation,
But keeps on blowing
Smoke rings into the air,
And silently watches the people of
every station
Coming and going
In and out of the alley and into the square.

I also suspect that he sometimes says
a prayer
For those that he nods to whenever they say
Hello;
And I also think this would be a nice
interpretation
Of Mr. McNally's odd and quiet vocation,
And very good for the people of our nation,
If this were so.

REBECCA

Rebecca, you continual sitter
And Knitter,
Within whose perpetual lap our
garments grow

We offer you this little rhyme to
let you Know
That though
Whatever we mention
Gets only half your attention,
And the other half, for worse or better
Is given to somebody's sweater;
Nevertheless,
I guess
That when the weather gets colder,
Some torso and arm and shoulder
Will warmer be,
Because of your chilly style of sociability.

THE SEXTON

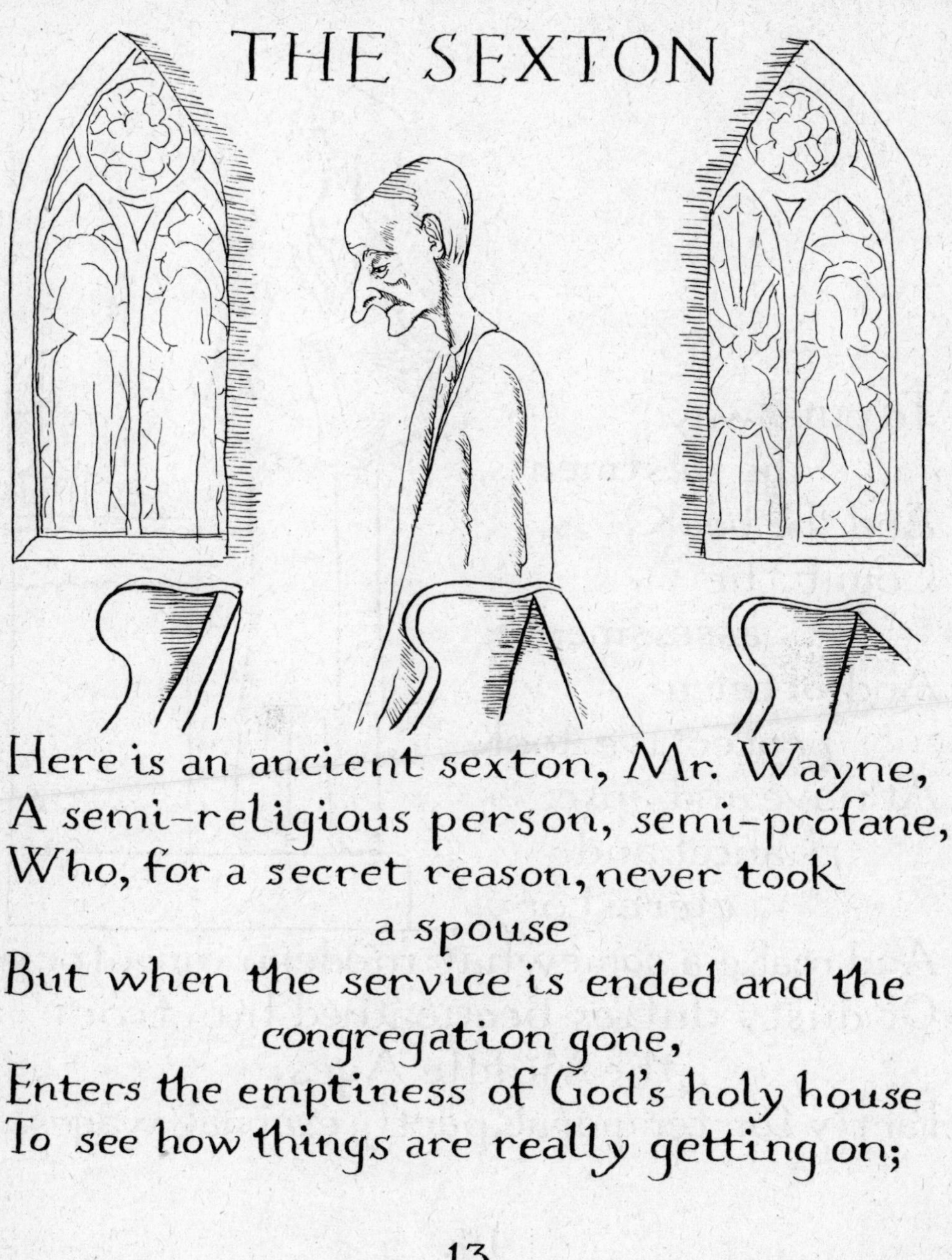

Here is an ancient sexton, Mr. Wayne,
A semi-religious person, semi-profane,
Who, for a secret reason, never took
a spouse
But when the service is ended and the
congregation gone,
Enters the emptiness of God's holy house
To see how things are really getting on;

To put away
the vestments,
And the book,
Count the
assessments,
And offer a
protective look
At nave and apse,
chancel and
clerestory,
And make a somewhat modern inventory
Of dusty duties bequeathed him from
the Middle Ages,
Partly for temporal, partly eternal wages.

THE OLD POSTMAN

Here's an old postman, now retired,
(For an old postman never gets fired);

And what has become of his jacket,
the lightest of blues?

It hangs in the closet.

And what has become of the good
and bad neighborhood news
He used to deposit?
It hangs in a bag on the back of a
younger and lesser

Lad, who will trudge his way to
retirement, step by step,
If he sticks it out as long as his
predecessor,
Through forty nine Fall elections,
Dem. and Rep.

MR. PLATER

Here is Mr. Plater,
A toothpick advocator
Who likes to point
from West

to East

to South,

In the course of conversation
After a good collation,
With a toothpick in his mouth.

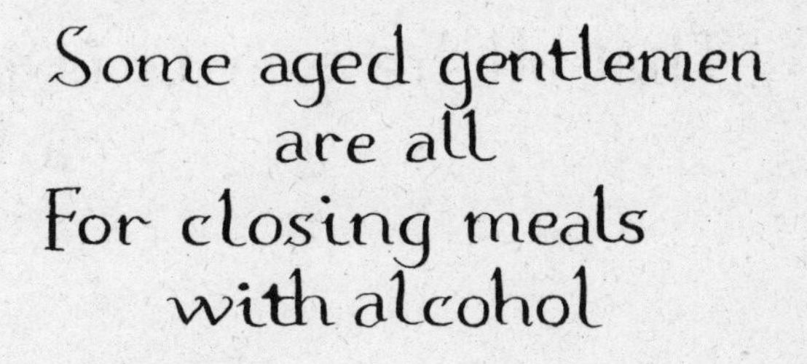

Some aged gentlemen
are all
For closing meals
with alcohol

But Plater
Makes it clearly understood,
When his repast is ended
And you see his arm extended
To the waiter,

That all he wants is just
a bit of wood.

MRS. BEVERLEY

Buxom Mrs. Beverley
Spends her afternoons
Pouring tea,
Dispensing saucers, cups and spoons
To a select company;
Making interminable queries:
Questions arranged in a series,
To each of which you must reply
While your palate still is dry.

Tea or coffee?
Tea.
India or China?
India.
Strong or weak?
Strong.
Half a cup, or full cup?
Full cup.
Cream or lemon?
Cream.
One lump, or two lumps?
Two lumps.
Then buxom Mrs. Beverley
Gives you what you asked for, gives you
tea,
And hopes it will restore the energy
You lost in being bored
By answering her questions while
she poured.

THE PROFESSOR

Here is old Professor Meade.
And there are the books he used to read.
And here's a picture of his study,
Before his memory and his mind went muddy
And here's the desk, and swivel chair
He sat in

Before he lost his eyesight and his hair
While settling for the human race
The problems of the dative case
In Latin.

And now behold the garden
He took to when his arteries
Began to harden.

And here he is upon his knees,

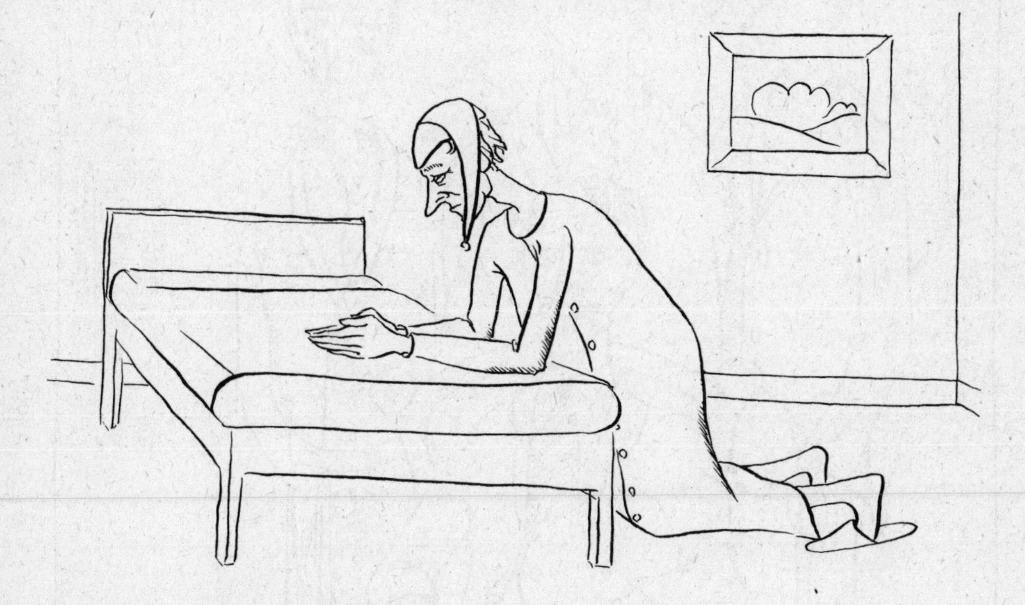

Asking God's pardon
For any academic slip
Committed in a life of scholarship,
The sort of intellectual misdeed
An angel might have made, were he
Professor Meade.

THE BRAGGY BROTHERS

Four aged bachelors are these:
The Braggy brothers,
Matrimonially difficult to please,
And therefore there will be no others;

No others with the Braggy name,
The Braggy fortune, Braggy fame,
No little boys with Braggy faults,
Like playing tag, or turning somersaults.

Their story ends up somewhat sad,
For ancestors were all they ever had.

ABIGAIL

Abigail is one to whom
All is gloom.
And when you meet her,
so you may assume.

There's no use trying to say:
"Now how did you get that way?
And don't you think this is
a lovely day?"

Blue skies remind her that it is apt
to rain.

Pleasure suggests pain,
And daylight that it will soon be
dark again.

"The best of efforts fail,
And life is just a vale
Of tears, my dears", says weepy Abigail.

GRANDMA GERTIE

Here is a glimpse of Gertrude,
better known as Grandma Gertie,

Who in the time of Grover Cleveland,
arrived at the age of thirty,
And who still retains under Roosevelt
a flair for being flirty.

(One can hear Grandma murmuring:
"Good gracious!
The epithet he wanted was *flirtatious*;
But poets with no urge for the sublime,
Will go to most any length to get a
rhyme.")

Poet resumes

Anything that is masculine has the
power to overcome her:
A sauntering policeman or a circum-
ambient plumber,
An old man selling shoestrings on the
sidewalk in the summer

(Here Grandma Gertie interrupts again.
"You mean I have a mania for men
Because I wink an eye or wave a fan
At some old cute old octogenarian?")

Poet again resumes

Advisors medical and moral, both have
tried to aid her,
And from such romantic antics have
endeavored to dissuade her,
But Gertie says she promised God
to stay the way he made her.

MRS. DUGAN DOWD O'DEA

Meet Mrs. Dugan Dowd O'Dea,

Three times a widow

(Hubert, Hugh
and
Harry),

And, as one by one her husbands passed
away,
She was, of course left free again to
marry,
And marry again she did without delay,
So much so that the organist could
not decide
Whenever he saw her come to church,
what tune to play;
Should it be Mendelssohn or Fauré?
The Wedding March, or something not
so gay,
Like *Requiem aeternam dona ei,*
Domine?

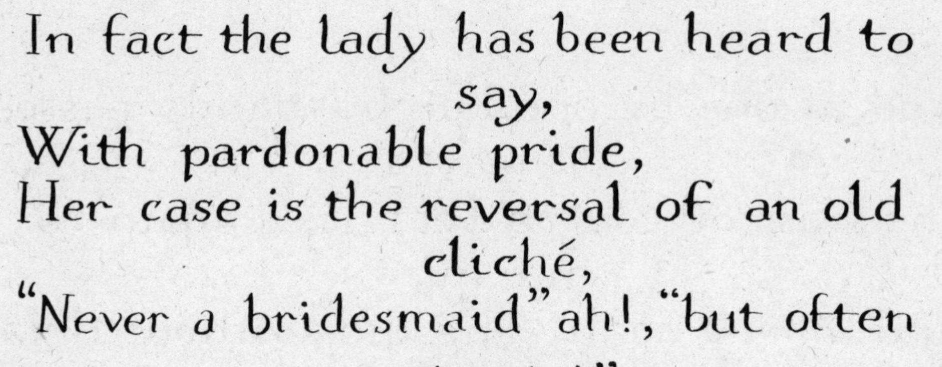

In fact the lady has been heard to
say,
With pardonable pride,
Her case is the reversal of an old
cliché,
"Never a bridesmaid" ah!, "but often
a bride!"

SOME OLD MEN

Some old men sit in the sun,
Some old men in the shade,

And it is haunting
When their work is done,
To see them sit and doze
In various attitudes of repose,
On drowsy doorstep or under
covered colonnade,
Each wondering if he is wanting
While waiting to be weighed.

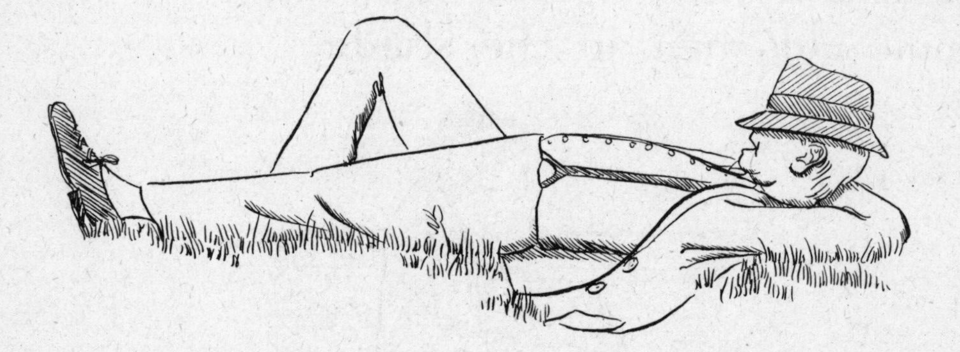

BERTHA

Behold old Bertha sitting desolate,
Endeavoring to meditate
Why certain senile women put on
weight.

Bertha insists: "It can't be what I ate,
Since Mrs. Casey, Mrs. Cummiskey,
and Mrs. Klein
All possess appetites as large as mine!"

"I guess it must be" says Bertha, "that
fullness is me fate,
'Cause every scale I stands on indicate
That some of me is framework, but
most of me is freight."

THE EDGERTONS

Seated on their verandah alongside
one another,
Here are Mrs. and Mr. Edgerton,
A ninety-four-year-old mother,
And a seventy-two-year-old son.

Naturally with folks as old as these,
It's hard to picture them as
mère et fils.

Some people say to HIM: "Your wife
Seems at her age to still have lots of
life!"

Some people say to HER: "I gather
You do enjoy the company of your
father!"

Some people say to BOTH of THEM:
"Now which is which, parentally? Ahem!"

While others with a yawn or a hiccup
Just give the whole thing up.

THE OLD NUNS

Here are some nuns at twilight,
old nuns who take the air
In conventual enclosure, just before
their evening prayer,
Of whom you do not see their ears,
or ever see their hair.

But their eyes are bathed in sunsets
that unfold above the hill,
And they hold the glory of God is
there, and the wonder of God's will,
Although some of them are not so well,
and some extremely ill.

But you do not hear a murmur, or a
moan, or a complaint
As they recreate at evening on the
benches old and quaint,
Each convinced she is a sinner,
and if God thinks each a saint,
You would never quite suspect it
to hear the old nuns talk,
In the shadows of the convent tower,
beside the garden walk,
While eternity keeps threatening
in the clicking of the clock.

THE HERMIT

Here is what happened to a queer
old hermit
Who poached on a farmer's property
without a permit.

The town officials who went out to find him.

Discovered only things he left behind him:
His jacket hanging on a bush, his foot-tracks in the clearance,

All sorts of various vestiges of his
sudden disappearance;
The walk he almost weeded, and
the wood he almost cut,
And the house he almost lived in,
that a hermit calls a hut.

AUNT KATE

Leave it to old Aunt
Kate,
Slow and deliberate,
No one was ever able
to hurry her.

Even the mourners and the undertaker
Had to wait,
The day they took her to God's acre
To bury her.

THE OLD ACTRESS

In histrionic lavender and lace,
Costumed from seasons long ago,
Before the footlights of a fireplace,
Lily, the actress dreams of what
she was,

And listens to the crackle of applause,
The while the burning logs put on
a show.

With curtailed gestures and with
hampered art,
That ague and rheumatism have
not greatly assisted,
She plays the small rôle of a half-
broken heart,
In which a leading lady has still
persisted,
And carries on whatever may befall,
Till the last curtain, minus the
curtain call.

OLD BILL

Here is old Bill Flynn.
All his hay is in.
All his hens are fed,
All his children wed.
All his bills are paid.

Arrangements have been made
To leave the old homestead
To his next of kin.

All his sins are shriven,
All his faults forgiven
Till seventy times seven.
All his enemies are dead,
And all his friends in Heaven.

FAREWELL TO MRS. SHIVVER

Entombed and epitaphed
Away from breeze and draught,

In grateful, willing chores
We closed ten thousand doors.
But no! The little chill
Went on persisting still.

She had no real disease.
A sniffle and a sneeze
Are symptoms, pray, of what?
Of anything you've got!

But what that was we know
No more than long ago,
When in we rushed and knelt
And felt how cold she felt,

And everyone agreed
There was no longer need
Of what we'd gladly do,
If she could want us to.